YOUR LAND AND MY LAND

We Visit

CHILE

Tamra

Orr

Mitchell Lane

P.O. Box 196
Hockessin, Delaware 19707

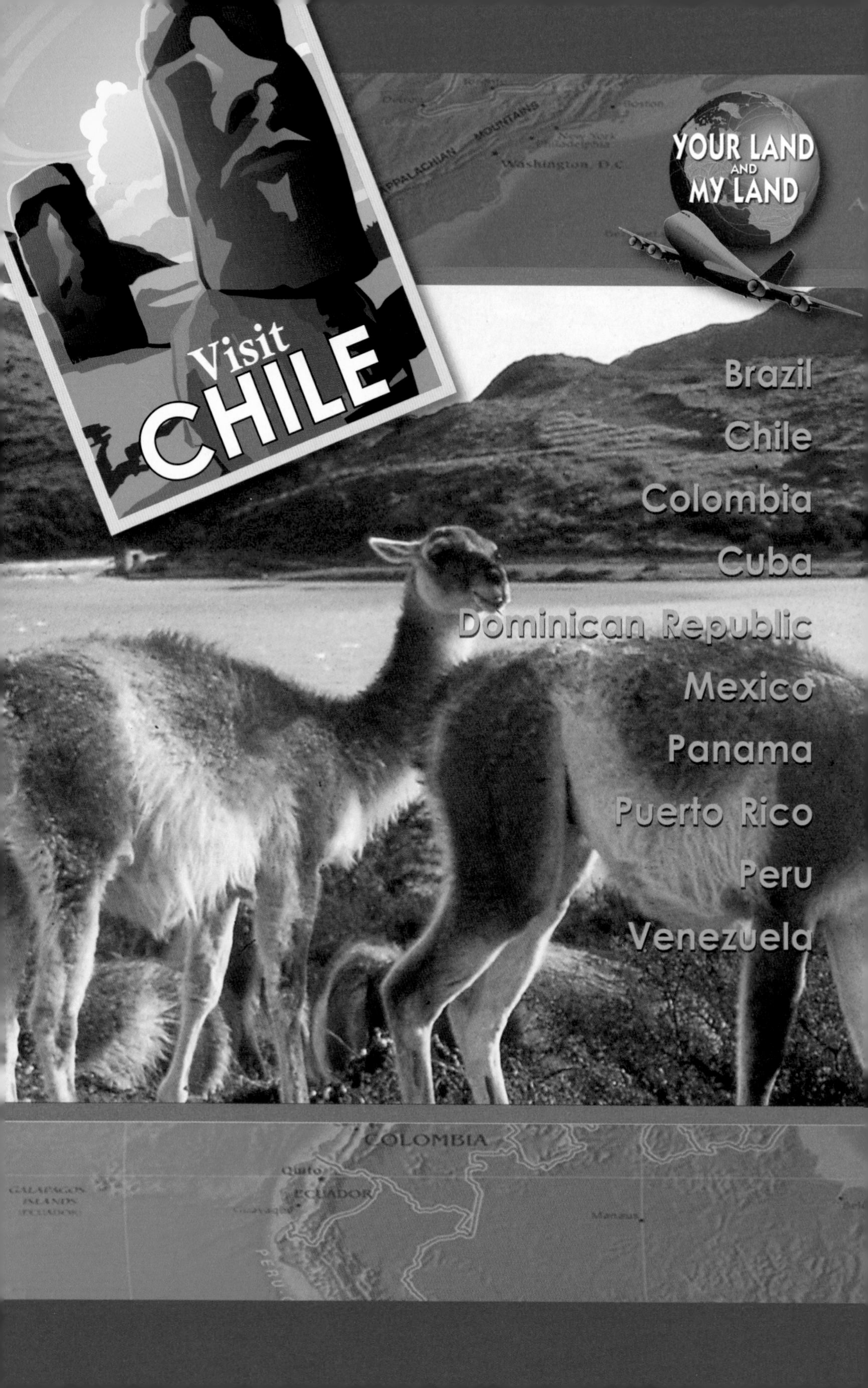

Visit
CHILE
YOUR LAND AND MY LAND
APPALACHIAN MOUNTAINS
Boston
Washington, D.C.
Brazil
Chile
Colombia
Cuba
Dominican Republic
Mexico
Panama
Puerto Rico
Peru
Venezuela
COLOMBIA
Quito
ECUADOR
Manaus

YOUR LAND
AND
MY LAND

We Visit

CHILE

Mitchell Lane
PUBLISHERS

Printing   1   2   3   4   5   6   7   8   9

Library of Congress Cataloging-in-Publication Data
Orr, Tamra.
  We visit Chile / by Tamra Orr.
     p. cm. — (Your land and my land)
  Includes bibliographical references and index.
  ISBN 978-1-58415-888-2 (lib. bdg.)
  1. Chile—Juvenile literature. I. Title.
  F3058.5.O77 2010
  983—dc22

                                                            2010006562

PUBLISHER'S NOTE: This story is based on the author's extensive research, which she believes to be accurate. Documentation of this research is on page 61.

    The Internet sites referenced herein were active as of the publication date. Due to the fleeting nature of some web sites, we cannot guarantee they will all be active when you are reading this book.

    To reflect current usage, we have chosen to use the secular era designations BCE ("before the common era") and CE ("of the common era") instead of the traditional designations BC ("before Christ") and AD (*anno Domini*, "in the year

Contents

Introduction

Can you find Latin America on the map or globe? Start by finding the United States. Go south to just below the states of California, Arizona, New Mexico, and Texas. Do you see Mexico? You have found the top of Latin America! See how closely it connects to the United States? Follow Mexico farther south. It and the Central American countries act like a long hook between the United States and the many other republics found in this area. Latin America is home to people who speak mainly Spanish, Portuguese, and French. More than two dozen exciting places are found there.

More than 500 million people live throughout Latin America. Most of them make their homes along the west coast and in the highlands of Mexico and the Andes Mountains. It is a region that is rich in history, culture, and amazing people. Let's explore one part of it, the Republic of Chile.

The Regions and Countries of Latin America

LATIN
AMERICA

Caribbean: Cuba, the Dominican Republic, French
West Indies, Haiti, and Puerto Rico
North America: Mexico
Central America: Belize, Costa Rica, El Salvador,
Guatemala, Honduras, Nicaragua, Panama
South America: Argentina, Bolivia, Brazil, Chile,
Colombia, Ecuador, French Guiana, Guyana,
Paraguay, Peru, Suriname, Uruguay,
Venezuela

Santiago is the capital of Chile and also its largest city. It is located in the country's central valley. Although it is the capital, the government meets in the coastal town of Valparaiso instead. It is located about two hours by car to the west.

Country Overview

Welcome to Chile! You might be surprised to know that Chile is the longest, skinniest country in the world. Look at the map. Do you see that long, thin country on the western coast of South America? It reaches all the way from the corners of Peru and Bolivia to the southern tip of Argentina. It is as long as the distance from San Francisco, California, to New York, New York. At its widest point, it is only 150 miles across. Can you imagine such a country and traveling all the way from one end of it to the other? The differences are dramatic.

How did such an oddly shaped country come to be? An old Chilean legend explains it this way: Long ago, after God created the world, he stopped and looked around. He was puzzled. Everything fit together so well, but there were a lot of little pieces left over. He had some lush forests, clear lakes, towering mountain ranges, and fertile plains that he simply did not know what to do with. Finally, he decided to stick all of them together in a chain and hang them right at the end of the world. It would make the longest country on earth. It would make Chile!

Chilean mask

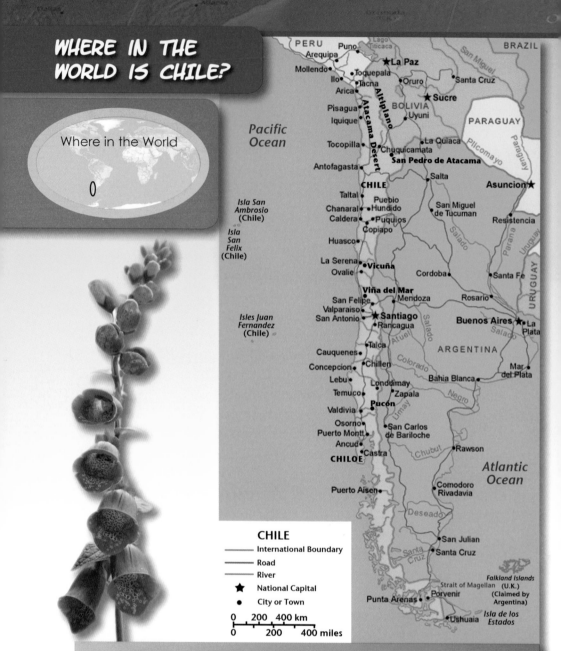

WHERE IN THE WORLD IS CHILE?

Where in the World

0

Chile (in peach) stretches along the Pacific coast of South America. It stretches so many miles that it has almost completely different climates, wildlife, and cultures from one end to the other. Along the coastline, a number of islands dot the ocean. Those are part of Chile, too. Patagonia is a region that covers southern Chile and Argentina.

CHILE FACTS AT A GLANCE

Official name: Republic of Chile

Capital: Santiago

Size: 291,931 square miles
(756,102 square kilometers)

Length: About 2,672 miles
(4,300 kilometers)

Land area: 287,186 square miles (743,812 square kilometers)

Copihue

Water area: 4,745 square miles (12,290 square kilometers)

Highest point: Nevado Ojos del Salado—22,572 feet (6,880 meters)

Lowest point: Beaches along Pacific Ocean—0 feet (0 meters)

Population: 16,601,707 (2009)

Ethnic groups: White and White-Amerindian 95.4%; Mapuche 4%

Languages: Spanish, Mapudungun, German, English

Exports: Copper, fish, paper and pulp, chemicals, wine, fruit

Imports: Petroleum and products, chemicals, electrical and tele-communications equipment, industrial machinery, vehicles, natural gas

Agricultural products: Fruit, wheat, corn, beef, poultry, wool, fish, timber

Flag: Chile's flag shows a band of white over a band of red. The white stands for snow in the Andes. The red stands for the blood of the Mapuches who fought against the Spanish. The blue square on the white band stands for Chile's clear blue sky. The white five-pointed star on the blue was used in the banners on battlefields and means "progress and honor."

National flower: Copihue (KOH-pee-way), also known as the Chilean bellflower

National bird: Andean c_ _or

Source: CIA World Factbook, Chile

FYI FACT: Chile is eighteen times longer than it is wide.

El Tatio Geysers, more than 13,000 feet (4,000 meters) above sea level, are in the region of Antofagasta. As the sun rises each cold morning, huge spurts of steam erupt from the ground through blowholes.

The Land of Extremes

Because Chile covers so many miles, a little of every type of climate can be found there. The north end of Chile is hot and tropical, while the south end is just short of the freezing Antarctic.

The eastern portion of Chile borders the Andes mountain range. This area has more than 2,000 volcanoes, many of which are still rumbling. The country's highest point is in this region. It is the Nevado Ojos del Salado (oh-HOHS del SAH-lah-do, or "Salty Eye"), a mountain peak that soars 22,572 feet (6,880 meters)—over 4.25 miles (6.8 kilometers)—toward the sky.

In Central Chile, where three quarters of the people live, the land features sand dunes and boiling geysers, salt flats and flat plains. This area also has the 1,200-square-mile (3,000-square-kilometer) Atacama Desert. This desert is one of the driest places in the world and is almost completely barren most of the time. Now and then, torrential rains will move through the area, especially if the weather is under the effect of El Niño. During this time, the desert is briefly submerged by flash floods. For just a few brief days, plants and flowers pop up—and then the heat and dry air wither them again.

The entire west side of Chile is ocean shore. Often called the Cordillera de la Costa (kor-dee-YAYR-ah deh lah KOHS-tah, meaning "mountain range of the coast"), it reaches from Arica in the far north

The Miscanti Lagoon is a heart-shaped lake in San Pedro de Atacama. The water in it is a deep turquoise blue. It has more salt in it than fresh water but less than the ocean.

Wulff Castle

The Atacama Desert has many astronomical observatories, including the Atacama Large Millimeter/Submillimeter Array (ALMA). It is so distant from any cities that there is no light pollution to spoil the view. By the end of 2011, the sixty-six 12-meter- and 7-meter-diameter radio telescopes will be operational. ALMA will be the largest radio telescope in the world.

to Puerto Montt in the south. This part of the country includes Chiloe, the largest of Chile's islands and the fifth largest island in South America. It is 118 miles (190 kilometers) from north to south and under 40 miles (64 kilometers) wide. A land of many small farms and dense forests, the island is often covered with a thick layer of ocean fog.

Viña del Mar, Chile

The Mapuche people have a rich history in Chile. They were a strong people who managed to survive attacks by the Incas. Even today, they have strong communities within Chile.

An Early History of Chile

Long, long ago, Chile was home to a few small groups of people who lived in different communities along the western coast of South America. The Aymara were in the north, the Atacameños and Diaguita in the central areas, and the Mapuche between Santiago and Patagonia. In the coldest parts of southern Patagonia, a handful of other small groups settled.

For centuries, the Mapuche group dominated the area. When foreigners such as the Incas tried to invade them, the Mapuche fought back—hard! Between 1450 and 1500, the Incas began marching across the country, but they were stopped and forced back by this hardy, determined group. In 1541, Pedro de Valdivia established the city of Santiago. The Mapuche burned down everything that had been built. In 1552, the group got a new leader, Lautaro. He taught his warriors how to fight more effectively and introduced them to battling from horseback. Within a year, the Mapuche had killed de Valdivia.

The battle for their land was not over, however. In the late sixteenth century, Spain was trying to take over large parts of Chile. Once again, the Mapuche refused to let them and pushed the Spanish back. For the next 250 years, the Mapuche kept control of Chile.

Gaining Independence

In the late eighteenth century, Spain sent large numbers of armed settlers into Chile and finally took control away from the Mapuche. By 1810, the *Criollos* (kree-OH-yohs—Spaniards who were born in Chile) were tired of being governed by outsiders and began fighting for their independence. Their first president was a half-Irish, half-Chilean man named Bernardo O'Higgins. Although he helped get Chile's first Declaration of Independence signed in 1818, it took years of fighting before Spain granted it in 1840.

In this 1945 painting, *Proclamación y jura de la Independencia de Chile (The Declaration of Independence of Chile)* by famous Chilean painter Pedro Subercaseaux, the people celebrate their first taste of independence and their new flag.

During the late nineteenth century, Chile continued to fight, this time against Peru and Bolivia in the War of the Pacific. When it was over, Chile had won a great deal of land, much of it rich with copper. Laborers continued to campaign for a leader who would represent their needs. That leadership did not last long, and it did not solve any of their problems. From 1920 to 1924, the country had a military government, but that came to an end

FYI FACT:

When a child's small footprint was found in Chile's Monte Verde region, it was estimated to be 12,500 years old. Other evidence determined that humans lived in this area as long ago as 33,000 years.

when the effects of the world financial depression reached Chile. By 1938, a new political group led by communists and socialists took over. That also came to an end when communism was outlawed throughout the country. A socialist president, Salvador Allende, followed, but once again, the people were not satisfied.

Worker Unrest

While copper helped bring far more money into Chile, at the same time it increased the tension between the country's wealthy and the poor who had rushed to the area to work in the mines. Workers began to protest, and two bloody battles were fought: the Meat Massacre (1904) and the Massacre of Escuela Santa Maria (1907) (*escuela*—es-KWAY-ah—means "school").

During World War I, the number of exports fell, and many Chileans lost their jobs. Unrest continued as the government tried to put

In 1964, workers marched through the streets in support of Allende. In the next presidential election, he narrowly won.

measures in place to improve the economy but not to improve workers' wages. Although groups of people tried to start a new government or solve Chile's problems, they were unsuccessful.

Between 1932 and 1938, the world depression had negative effects in Chile, as in most countries. Unemployment went up and exports went down. President Arturo Alessandri made it his top priority to turn things around, and while he was able to improve things, his efforts were not enough.

The next leader, Pedro Aguirre Cerda, focused on making Chile less dependent on importing what it needed from other countries by creating more of what it needed on its own. Under Allende's control (1970–1973), Chile suffered an economic crisis like it had never seen before—but even worse was in store.

President Pedro Aguirre Cerda

Army General Augusto Pinochet left quite a legacy in Chile—but it was not an honorable one. His years in power were some of the worst and darkest times in the country's entire history.

Chapter 4

A Changing History

In 1973, Army General Augusto Pinochet (PEE-noh-shay) raided the presidential offices. President Salvador Allende died in the battle. Under Pinochet's leadership, Chile's economy shifted to a free market economy, which means that people could make whatever they wanted and choose how much to charge for it. At the same time, Chile suffered its highest levels of unemployment in its history, and growing numbers of people had to deal with poverty.

For the next sixteen years, Pinochet controlled the Chilean people—and it was a long and pain-filled time. More than 3,000 people were killed or simply disappeared under his rule, or they were sent away in exile. Companies and workers were not allowed to strike. He controlled what was written and said about him in the press. He also organized his own group of secret police, known as the National Intelligence Directorate, or DINA. They carried out his orders—whatever they happened to be. Pinochet remained in power until 1989 when growing economic problems led to intense unrest and protests spilling onto the streets. He was taken out of office, and Patricio Aylwin was elected in the country's first free elections in more than twenty years.

Chile was not rid of the dictator yet. Pinochet became the head of the armed forces, and then got himself elected senator for life. In 1998, he was arrested in London for suspicion of "crimes against humanity," including murders and disappearances. However, because of his poor health, he was returned to Chile and all charges were dropped. When he died in 2006 from complications of a heart attack, many people rejoiced.

The same year, Chile got its first female president, Michelle Bachelet. Ironically, she had once been one of Pinochet's political prisoners. While she was studying to be a doctor, she was arrested, along with the rest of her family. She and her mother were sent to a secret prison where they were tortured, before finally being released into exile in 1975. The two of them lived in Australia and East Germany until 1979. Then, Bachelet returned to Chile and graduated from medical

Before she became president of Chile, Michelle Bachelet was Minister of Defense. She was a popular president. On the day she left office in 2010, women from all over the country came to honor her by waving white handkerchiefs and shouting for her to run for president again in 2014.

school as a surgeon. She was also quite involved in politics, and by 1996 she was running for local offices. In 2000, she was named Minister of Health. She worked hard to bring better health care to all Chileans by improving public health clinics and reducing the waiting time for treatment. Two years later, she was named Minister of Defense, the first woman in Latin America to earn this position.

The next election for president was held in December 2009. Neither of the candidates, Sebastián Piñera or Eduardo Frei, received the majority of votes and a runoff was held January 17, 2010. In that election, Piñera won by a small margin.

President Sebastián Piñera

Chilean vineyard in the Andes foothills

A Strong Economy

After the year 2000, Chile's economy began to get stronger, due to its production of copper and to its variety of crops. Chileans produce sugar, beans, potatoes, beets, and wheat. They also have quite a few vineyards that are recognized as excellent sources for wine.

A main factor in its economy is its copper mining. Chile is the world's largest copper producer and has been since the 1860s. It produces more than 35 percent of the copper shipped and used throughout the world. Almost half of all its exports is copper.

FYI FACT:

Copper is most commonly used for electrical wiring. It is also used in copper pipes and tubes, as well as on kitchen pans.

The Chuquicamata mine is so huge that it can be seen from space. Until the 1990s, it was Chile's largest mine, but it has been replaced by the Escondida copper mine, which is 3,280 feet (1,000 meters) deep and almost 10,000 feet (3,000 meters) wide. Each day huge, rumbling trucks with 13-foot- (4-meter-) tall tires file down into the mine to take out loads of rocks. Each year, more than 590,000 tons (536,000 metric tons) of copper is taken out of this mine.

Satellite image of Escondida Copper Mine

Humberstone was once a booming town during the nitrate boom of the late 1800s. By the middle of the twentieth century, it was a ghost town. In 2010, it was an official historical site and was undergoing renovations.

From One End
to the Other

Chile stretches over so much country that there is a wide range of climates, flora, and fauna within its borders. At the top of the country, next to Peru, it is tropical and sunny. At the very bottom, it is far different.

Stop in north Chile to see the ghost town of Humberstone 28 miles (45 kilometers) east of Iquique. In the late nineteenth century, it was a bustling city full of miners, but seventy years later, there was little left to see but crumbling equipment and ramshackle houses. In 2005, it was declared a World Heritage Site, and restorations began shortly after.

Halfway down the country, almost right in the middle, is Chile's largest city, Santiago. Founded in 1541 by the Spanish conquistador Pedro de Valdivia, it has grown to become the fifth-largest city in South America. Approximately 6 million people—one-third of the nation's population—live there. It is a beautiful, modern city with vineyards, beaches and museums, glaciers and hot springs, as well as places like the National Museum of Fine Arts and the Palacio de la Moneda (pah-LAH-the-oh de la moh-NAY-dah—"palace of money"). Each day the Central Market draws natives and tourists alike. They watch the fresh catches of fish come in from the ocean and see who can get the best price for them.

On the northern side of Santiago is Viña del Mar. There you can find the Jardin Botanico Nacional (har-DEEN boh-TAH-nee-koh nah-the-oh-NAHL, the National Botanical Gardens), with more than 150 acres (60 hectares) of native, exotic, and endangered plants. This region includes the popular tourist attractions of Playa Acapulco and Mirasol. Viña del Mar attracts people from all over the world to see its white sandy beaches, or to take a horse-drawn carriage ride through its quaint streets.

Viña del Mar's Reloj de Flores (flower clock) is made entirely of live flowers and plants and still manages to tell the correct time. In the center is a huge timepiece that was donated by Switzerland in 1962 during the World Cup games.

Not far from this city is Valparaiso, or Valpo, as it is called locally. One of the most unusual cities in all of Chile, Valpo has many steep hills. To cope with them, it has a system of *ascensores,* or train-like elevators. Inside, fifteen cable cars that are connected to pulleys on each end ride up and down on train tracks. Each trip takes only a couple of minutes and carries passengers directly to their individual neighborhoods. More than three million people ride in them every year.

Concepción is a port city on the central coast. It is the site of many of Chile's universities and shopping malls.

To the south is the Temuco region, home to the Mapuche, the largest indigenous group left in Chile. It is part of the Lake District, an area that features rolling hills, thick forests, and volcanic peaks topped with snow. The Mapuche—"People of the Land"—number about 600,000. In Temuco, most of

Riding the *ascensores* is quite an experience. It costs less to ride down than to ride up, and fees are collected at the end of the ride.

them make a living by farming or fishing. The other major ethnic group in Chile is the Aymara. Most of them live in the coastal cities.

The people who live on the coast are constantly aware that they live in danger. On May 22, 1960, Chile had what is still considered the largest earthquake of the twentieth century. With a magnitude of

9.5, it not only shook and destroyed buildings and homes, but it also triggered a tsunami reported to be more than 70 feet (21 meters) tall.

Before the major quake, the earth rumbled a few times, sending people outside and into the street to see what was happening. This factor helped save lives. When the main quake hit, many of the buildings were far emptier than they might have been. Those who jumped into their boats and went to sea for protection, however, were all lost when the tsunami came through minutes later. Between the two disasters, thousands of people perished, and billions of dollars' worth of damage was done.

In February 2010, another earthquake struck Chile. This one measured 8.8 on the Richter scale. Hundreds of people perished, and a tsunami warning was issued throughout the Pacific, all the way to Oregon and Washington in the United States. Aid came from all over the world to help the Chileans, but experts estimated it would take years before the country would recover.

The southern portion of Chile is often called Patagonia. Much of it is so remote that the only way to get to it is by airplane or through Argentina. There are no roads that directly connect Patagonia with the rest of Chile. Locally it is referred to as El Fin del Mundo (el-FEEN del MOON-doh), or The End of the World. Although some people live there, farms are isolated and far apart. The scenery is beautiful. It offers waterfalls, mountaintops, lagoons, and lakes. Visitors come to see rain forests or stop by the 1,160-square-mile (1,871-square-kilometer) Parque Pumalin (PAR-kay PUH-muh-lin), the largest private nature reserve in the world. You can spot some of Chile's most colorful flowers there, along with the indigenous alerce tree. Like the California redwood, these trees can live for centuries. On Pata-

Zapatito de la Virgen (Virgin's slipper), Parque Nacional Torres del Paine

gonia's river Futaleufú (foo-tuh-LYOO-foo), thousands of rafting and kayaking fans come to wend their way through some of the planet's most exciting rapids.

Hundreds of thousands of people also go to Southern Patagonia. Over 200,000 tourists go through the Parque Nacional Torres del Paine (National Park of the Paine Towers), South America's number one park. Some come for the glaciers, while others come to see 9,000-foot- (2,700-meter-) tall granite pillars.

Nature lovers will want to stop by Southern Patagonia to see the multiple penguin colonies there. One of the islands in the region features

The Parque Nacional Torres del Paine (Park of the Towers of Paine) is a popular place for hiking and mountain climbing. Photos of the granite pillars are often used on posters and book covers.

Besides emerald green forests, roaring rivers, and hidden lakes, Parque Nacional Torres del Paine has glowing blue glaciers. Since 1978, the park has been part of UNESCO's Biosphere Reserve system.

Chilean Rockhopper Penguin

the Monumento Natural de los Pingüinos (pin-GWEE-nohs; Natural Monument of the Penguins). More than 100,000 penguins nest there between October and March. Visitors get the best view of the colonies from a 1902 lighthouse on the island.

Out on the Islands

Chile also features a number of islands farther out in the water, including Chiloe, Easter Island, the Juan Fernández Islands, and Tierra del Fuego (tee-AYR-ah del FWAY-goh, "Land of Fire"), plus many uninhabited isles. Chiloe is an interesting stop, as it includes 40 different islands, one of which is called Castro. It features houses built on stilts that almost appear to float on top of the

Juan Fernández Firecrown

water when the tide comes in. Tierra del Fuego is shared between Chile and Argentina and is home primarily to sheep farms and bird colonies. The Juan Fernández Islands are a tiny island chain where people stop by to see the wildlife, including the fur seal and Juan Fernández hummingbird. Every now and then a tourist may pause at one of the largest islands of the bunch. It is where Alexander Selkirk was marooned for four years; his story inspired Daniel Defoe to write his classic novel *Robinson Crusoe.*

Perhaps the most famous of Chile's islands is Rapa Nui, a Polynesian name. Most of the world knows it as Easter Island—the name bestowed on it by the Dutch explorer who discovered it on Easter Day in 1722. The island is 2,500 miles (4,000 kilometers) from the capital of Santiago and has three volcanoes on it. Without a doubt, what makes this island stand out from any others is the hundreds of *moai,* or volcanic rock figures, that are found there. Some are standing; others have fallen over and become broken over time. Some of them are mounted on an *ahu,* or stone platform. Exactly who built them—and moreover, *how* they built them—is still a mystery. The statues are huge, and some weigh as much as 82 tons. It would have taken up to 250 people to move one into position. The statues have been studied for years and have even appeared in movies such as *Night at the Museum.*

moai

Watching the Wildlife

Some of the world's oddest and most interesting creatures are found in parts of Chile. Over 100 species of birds fly overhead, including flamingos and eagles. Andean condors with wingspans that can reach over ten feet (three meters) are here, as well as two types of penguins. A flightless, ostrich-like bird called the rhea also calls Chile home.

A number of unusual mammals live in this region of the world. The guanaco is similar to a llama or alpaca, but it has a longer neck and thinner legs. A large type of puma is in Chile, along with the pudú, a small, shy deer. Of course, the waterways and oceans around Chile also support many species, including quite a few types of dolphins and whales.

From one end of the nation to the other are hundreds of plants, trees, bushes, and flowers. Some are found throughout Latin America,

The flamingos in Chile are large birds—standing four to five feet tall, with long necks and legs. They are able to lock their ankles and stand on one leg for long periods of time. This allows them to conserve heat. Flamingos make deep, honking sounds and can also grunt and howl.

The pudú is the tiniest deer in the world. Because of its size, it has to be very aware of predators in the area. If a pudú feels threatened, it runs in a zigzag pattern to get away. In some cases, it can even climb a tree to get to safety.

while others are just in particular parts of Chile. The *camanchaca* (kah-mahn-CHAH-kah), or ocean mist, that covers large parts of the country keeps things growing. Parts of Chile are actually the stormiest and wettest places on the entire planet. On the other hand, parts of the desert qualify as the driest.

Chile is an amazing country full of beautiful scenery, lively cities, fascinating creatures, and pretty plants. No matter where you turn, there is something to see and enjoy.

FYI FACT:

In 2005, 2.2 million tourists visited Chile. While many of them came from other parts of Latin America, European and Canadian visits also increased.

Schoolchildren from Punta Arenas listen to NASA scientist Dr. David Imel discuss the Airborne Synthetic Aperture Radar (AirSAR), which is used to study global warming in Patagonia and other parts of the world.

Meet the Chileans

It does not take long for the visitor to Chile to see that family is very important to Chileans. Children are truly cherished in the Chilean society. Babies and small children are often in arms. Hugs and kisses are handed out lavishly. Children and teenagers spend more time with their parents, grandparents, aunts, and uncles than in other cultures. Days are spent together, and on the holidays and weekends, relatives gather in one home to celebrate and relax. It is not unusual for young people to go directly from their childhood home to their married one.

There are more than 16 million people living throughout Chile. Almost all of them are white or white-Amerindian, a blend of white and Native American. Their background is more European than Latin American. They blend Spanish history with German influences, as well as Welsh, Irish, and others.

At Home

There are all kinds of homes in Chile because it covers so much area. There are huge mansions, some of which are historical and open for tours. Some of the wealthiest people live in fancy villas that include luxuries from tennis courts to swimming pools. There are countless apartment houses, with more being built all the time. Some areas have homes made out of adobe, a mix of mud and straw. Many homes have colorful tiles and are painted in bright colors.

Food plays a big role in the Chilean culture. Almost all holidays feature special recipes and family feasts. Breakfast, or *desayuno* (des-ah-YOO-noh), is a very light meal, usually consisting of milk or tea and perhaps some toast and jam. Lunch, or *almuerzo* (al-moo-AYR-thoh), is the largest meal of the day, taken between one and three in the afternoon. It often includes two main dishes: a salad with onions and tomatoes, followed by a beef or chicken dish served with vegetables. In late afternoon, usually between four and six, a snack called *once* (ON-thay) is served. It often includes bread, jam, cheeses, and avocados. Dinner or *cena* (THAY-nah) is typically eaten late, between nine and eleven P.M. It is usually a light meal as well, often consisting of little more than a sandwich.

Many people drink a bitter tea drink called *mate* (mah-TAY). It is usually served in a gourd, with a metal straw called a *bombilla* (bom-BEE-yah) inserted into it. Desserts are also quite popular throughout Chile. Some of the favorites include Italian-style ice cream called *helados* (ay-LAH-dohs), much like gelato. *Churros* (CHOOR-ohs), or fried treats, are filled with creamy vanilla or chocolate pudding. *Sopapillas* (soh-pah-PEE-yahs) are squares of fried dough covered in honey or sugar. Some vendors fry and sell them on the city streets.

Mate *in a gourd with a bombilla*

Churros *with chocolate dipping sauce*

At School

Like most other places in the world, Chilean children go to school each weekday. They begin at the age of six. They are in a primary school until the age of fourteen, and then they switch to another school until they graduate at age eighteen. Most begin their school day at 8:30 and end at 4:30. The school year in Chile begins in the middle of March and goes until the middle of December—their summer break is during the hot months between December and March. Most of the students are required to wear uniforms.

Since Chile is part of Latin America, it makes sense that the people speak Spanish, and this is the language taught in schools. While the language is the same, the accents and slang terms change slightly from one area to the next. Some refer to the language as *Chileno,* a combination of Spanish with input from German and the Mapuche. Words that are used only in Chile are sometimes called Chilenisms. One of them, *el taco,* means "traffic jam."

In Church

Most Chileans are Catholic. They celebrate many of the Catholic holidays and attend Catholic mass on a regular basis. Their faith guides many of their daily decisions and attitudes. For example, divorce became legal in the country only in 2004.

These two dancers are participating in the *cueca*, a dance that imitates the courting ritual of a rooster and a hen. While the male dancers chase the females, the females try to get away or even fight back!

Culture and Lifestyle

If you see people greet each other in Chile, you may see a great deal of touching. Men who don't know each other well will most likely shake hands, but good friends are likely to hug and pat each other on the back. Women pat each other on the right forearm or shoulder if they have met only a few times, but family members will kiss each other on the right cheek. They often do this when saying hello and good-bye.

As a guest at mealtime, you may notice that Chileans are rather formal (polite!). Women typically are seated before men. No one starts eating until the host invites them to do so. No one drinks until a toast is made. The most common toast to make is *"Salud!"* which means "to your health."

When eating a meal, they always keep their hands where they can be seen, with their wrists resting on the edge of the table. And though they use a fork and knife or spoon to eat, they don't talk until they put their silverware down.

Time to Dance

Chileans tend to work hard, but they rarely let their jobs come before family. Weekends and holidays are spent with family, and it is very unusual for anyone to work overtime. As hard as they work, they also enjoy celebrating and going to parties. They often do the *cueca* (koo-

Lapis lazuli elephant

FYI FACT:

Chile is gaining a reputation for its lapis lazuli, a semiprecious gemstone found in mines such as the Flor de los Andes (Flower of the Andes) in the Ovalle Mountains. These light-and-dark-blue stones are used in all kinds of jewelry and are sold in tourist shops throughout the country.

AY-kah), Chile's national dance, accompanied by a guitar, tambourine, and accordion. The movements of the dance mimic the courtship between a man and a very difficult woman who keeps refusing his advances. Each dancer holds a handkerchief that he or she uses to emphasize gestures.

On Easter Island, the people enjoy completely different dances. They are called the *sau sau* and the *ula ula.* In many ways they are like the hula dances in Hawaii. Dancers wear flower necklaces and use their hips and arms to show meaning.

The Culture of the Mapuche

Although the Mapuche make up only about 4 percent of Chile's population, they still have a very strong influence on the country's culture and traditions. One of the most honored people within the Mapuche community is the *Machi*. The *Machi* is always a woman, and she is a spiritual healer. She often knows a great deal about natural healing, such as using drums and herbs for curing illnesses, plus she has been trained in the arts of weather prediction, dream interpretation, and warding off evil. Many of the Mapuche hang on to ancient beliefs about the forces of nature.

The Mapuche have a legend about how the world was created. The spirits of the Earth and Sea were at battle in the shape of snakes. One of them, Cai-Cai, threatened to raise all the oceans and flood the land.

44

Although the *Machi* is sometimes described as a good witch, she has an important role within the Mapuche community. Her training is done by apprenticing with an old *Machi*, who shares her knowledge on everything from how to tell what the weather will be like to how to keep evil away from your door.

The other spirit, Ten-Ten, rushed to tell the people to get to higher ground so that they would be safe. To help them, he created mountains with peaks that soared into the clouds. Then he turned his people into birds so that they could fly to safety. Those who could not escape turned into fish and stones.

Chilean poet Gabriela Mistral receives the Nobel Prize for Literature from King Gustav of Sweden on December 20, 1945, in Sweden.

Famous Chileans

Chile is known for producing a variety of artists, including Nobel Prize–winners and popular television entertainers. Here are a few of the country's most recognized celebrities.

Gabriela Mistral (1889–1957). As one of Chile's Nobel Prize–winners (in literature, 1945), Gabriela Mistral was the pen name for Lucila Godoy y Alcayaga. Born in Vicuña, she was the daughter of a poet. She began writing poetry while she was teaching school and continued writing for most of her life. She was an important person in Chile's educational system and was a consul for Chile in the European cities of Naples, Madrid, and Lisbon. Mistral's books of poems were published from 1914 through 1938. Most of her verses centered on love and loss. She was the first female Latin American poet to win the Nobel Prize for Literature. On her tombstone, it reads, "What the soul is to the body, so is the artist to his people."

Pablo Neruda (1904–1973). Another Chilean Nobel Prize–winner for literature (1971), Pablo Neruda's real name was Neftali Ricardo Reyes Basoalto. Born in Parral, he met Mistral when he was a child. The

Pablo Neruda

Isabel Allende

two became friends, and he began writing poetry. His first book was published in 1924. Neruda did a great deal of traveling for the Chilean government—he was the consul to Burma at age twenty-three. Much of his work centered on political and social issues. When his poetry spoke out against the Chilean president, Neruda was forced to live underground for two years. During the course of his lifetime, he wrote hundreds of poems.

Isabel Allende (b. 1942). Born in Lima, Peru, this popular author was raised by her grandparents in Santiago. Isabel Allende was brought up in a household that was full of books and storytelling. She graduated from high school at age sixteen and began working as a newspaper journalist and television interviewer. Everything in Allende's life changed in 1973. Her uncle, the president of Chile, was assassinated. Fearing for her safety, she and her family fled to Venezuela. After she moved there, she began writing novels, many of them based on her experiences in Chile. Over the years, a number of her books have been bestsellers, such as *Eva Luna* and *Daughter of Fortune*. A few have been made into movies, including *The House of the Spirits* and *Of Love and Shadows*.

Arturo Valenzuela (b. 1944). A professor and director of the Center for Latin American Studies at Georgetown University in Washington, D.C., Arturo Valenzuela worked for U.S. President Bill Clinton. He was part of National Security Affairs and acted as Director for the Inter-American Affairs at the National Security Council. Born in Concepción, he left Chile as a teenager, following the 1960 earthquake. In 2009, U.S. President Barack Obama nominated him Assistant Secretary of State for Western Hemisphere Affairs. In this position, Valenzuela advises the Secretary of State on diplomatic issues in other countries.

José Santos (b. 1961). When Chilean-born José Santos was a little boy, he knew he loved horses, so he began working as a groom to earn money. His father, a former jockey, taught him how to ride. He won his first horse race at the age of fifteen. He continued to win many races and then, in 1985, he moved to the United States and became the leading rider in New York. Santos won more than 4,000 times and earned more than $188 million. During his

Jockey José Santos returns to the winner's circle with Funny Cide after winning the 128th Preakness at Pimlico Race Track on May 17, 2003.

years on horseback, he had a few serious accidents. In 2007, a fall resulted in five fractured vertebrae, broken ribs, and more. He wore a body cast for months and retired from the racing business.

Cecilia Bolocco (b. 1965). A former beauty contest winner (Miss Universe 1987), Cecilia Bolocco was born in Santiago. She started her career as a dancer and fashion model and then moved to television and Spanish soap operas. After leaving Chile, she moved to the United States and worked as a news anchor for Spanish CNN. She won an Emmy for her talk shows, and then became a fixture in Chile when

Jorge Garcia

she married Carlos Menem, former president of Argentina. They divorced several years later. She continued as a fashion designer and mother.

Jorge Garcia (b. 1973). Although Jorge Garcia was born in Omaha, Nebraska, his father was Chilean and his mother was Cuban. He grew up in southern California. When he landed the role as a villain in his school's seventh-grade musical, his musical number brought down the house. At that moment, he realized that acting might be a great profession for him. By the time he was out of college, he was working as a standup comedian. He acted in a number of stage plays and commercials before landing the role of Hugo "Hurley" Reyes on the popular television series *Lost*.

Santiago Cabrera (b. 1978). Santiago Cabrera, an actor, was born in Venezuela but raised in Toronto, Madrid, London, and Romania because his father was a diplomat and had to do a great deal of traveling. Cabrera originally planned to become a soccer player and was given a scholarship to do so. He even went to the point of playing on a semi-pro team. It was his second passion that determined his future, however. He was given a role on the British television series *MI-5* and then in the miniseries *Empire*. When he won

Santiago Cabrera

the role of Isaac Mendez on the series *Heroes,* his fame also spread in the United States.

Fernando Francisco González (b. 1980). A professional tennis player, Fernando Francisco Gonzalez was born in Santiago. Over his years on the court, he has earned a number of nicknames,

Fernando González

including *La Reina Bomber* (The Queen Bomber—after the commune where he was born), Stone Hand, and Gonzo. Thanks to the influence of his father, who was an amateur tennis player, Gonzalez has been playing the game since he was six years old. Within a few years, he was living and training in the United States. Before he graduated from high school, he was rated the number one player in the world. He won the U.S. Open, the French Open, and the Davis Cup—all before he turned eighteen years old. In 1999, he became a professional and has been playing in major world tournaments ever since.

The Fiestas Patrias is a popular holiday through-out Chile. Each town has its own way of celebrating, from dance contests to kite flying competitions, rodeos to cooking contests.

Time to Celebrate!

The people of Chile celebrate a lot of the same holidays as many other countries, such as Christmas, New Year's, and Easter. They celebrate Halloween and Independence Day, as most nations do, plus, since so much of the country is Catholic, they also have important Catholic holidays, such as All Saints' Day, Immaculate Conception, and Maundy Thursday.

On December 31, Chile welcomes the start of a new year with late-night dinners and parties. Millions of people come to watch fireworks at midnight, sent up over the ocean.

February brings the Carnaval de Putre (KAR-nuh-val deh POOT-ray) in Altiplano. It features loud music, colorful costumes, and a game where children toss balloons filled with flour at each other. When a balloon breaks, it is quickly clear who was standing closest to it! In the same month, at the Valdivia waterfront, people gather to celebrate Noche de Valdivia. Dozens of boats float across the water. Each is decorated like a float in a parade, and thousands come to watch them go by. February also brings out hundreds of athletes who want to participate in the Ironman International Triathlon held in Pucón. This grueling competition involves swimming 1.2 miles in the waters of Lake Villarrica, bicycling 56 miles over the hilly roads to Argentina, and running 13.1 miles across the difficult paths of Pucón's peninsula.

In Chile, the rodeo is a popular attraction for Chileans and guests.

Sports fun continues in March with the National Rodeo Championship. Rodeos were declared the national sport of Chile in 1962. People flock to the corrals, or *media luna* (MAy-de-ah LOON-ah; "half moon") to watch their favorite riders and horses compete. Music and dancing create a backdrop to the festivities. Delicious food smells fill the air. In one event, riders wear bright ponchos and sashes and large decorated cowboy hats. Their black leather boots shine in the sun. Even the horses are dressed up. Finally, a steer is sent into the corral. The goal is to see how quickly and elegantly the horse and rider can pin the steer against the side of the arena three times. Points are given for form and style.

May 1 is Day of the Worker. It has been an official holiday since 1931. Public places close and everyone is given a day off. It is held in memory of the Haymarket Massacre in Chicago, Illinois, in 1886 when police shot at workers who were striking for shorter working days.

Summertime brings Fiestas Patrias (fee-ES-tas pah-TREE-ahs; Festival of the Home Country), the celebration of Independence Day and Armed Forces Day. Events range from folk dances and parades to rodeos and sack races. Many people go to *fondas* (boarding houses), buildings made with palm leaf roofs, and they eat empanadas, drink wine, and dance the *cueca*. A number of fishing villages also celebrate San Pedro, the patron saint of fishermen.

Christmastime is largely based on Catholic traditions. Many families go to Midnight Mass on Christmas Eve, and then go home to open presents. On Christmas Day, they gather for outdoor barbecues or head to the beach or closest pool. (Remember, in countries that are below the equator, the weather is warm at Christmas!) Most of the stores and other businesses shut down for the day so that everyone can spend time with their families rather than working. Viejito Pascuero (vee-ay-EE-toh pas-koo-AYR-oh) comes in his sleigh to bring presents, and families decorate Christmas trees. A drink called *cola de mono* (KOH-lah de MOH-noh), or monkey's tail, is prepared for adults to enjoy. It is made from coffee, milk, cinnamon, sugar, and alcohol. No matter what time of year you visit Chile, there is sure to be music, dancing, plenty of wildlife to see, and people to meet.

Quinoa Vegetable Soup

For more than 5,000 years, quinoa (KEEN-wah) has been grown in the mountains of South America. It was used in many different recipes. It was even used as a medicine to put on wounds and as soap. The seed comes in a variety of colors, from bright white to shades of red and even black. Quinoa is not only easy to use but is also quite nutritious. It is rich in calcium, iron, and several vitamins, and it is unusually high in protein.

Here is a simple, healthy recipe based on quinoa that you and an adult helper can make. Preparation time is 35 minutes. Cooking time is 25 minutes.

Ingredients

1 tablespoon vegetable oil
⅔ cup quinoa
1 carrot, diced
1 stalk celery, diced
½ onion, chopped
½ green bell pepper, chopped
2 cloves garlic, crushed
2 15-ounce cans chicken broth
 (or vegetable broth)
3½ cups water
2 large tomatoes, chopped
¼ head cabbage, chopped
Salt and pepper to taste

Instructions

1 Have an adult heat the vegetable oil in a large pot
 on medium heat.
2 Stir in the quinoa, carrot, celery, onion, bell
 pepper, and garlic.
3 Cook for a few minutes until ingredients are
 slightly browned. Stir often.
4 Pour in the broth, water, tomatoes, and cabbage.
5 Have an adult turn the heat up to high and bring
 to a boil.
6 Reduce heat to medium.
7 Simmer until the quinoa and vegetables are
 tender. This should take about 10 minutes.
8 Season with salt and pepper.
9 Scoop into bowls and enjoy!

Quinoa growing

Make Your Own Rain Stick

In South America, the rain stick is often called the *palos de agua* (pah-lohs de AHG-wah; stick of water). The indigenous people traditionally make them in order to talk to the rain spirits. The people living in the desert region of Chile usually use cactus spines to make them. They hammer the spines inside the cactus tube and then let it dry in the sun. Next, pebbles are added, and each end is sealed with pieces of wood. As the Chileans turn the rain stick from end to end, the pebbles drop through, making a sound like a gentle rain.

You can make your own rain stick with an adult's help.

Materials
Cardboard tube from inside a roll of
    wrapping paper
Marker
30 one-inch nails
Tape (masking tape or packing tape is best)
Scissors
Construction paper
Dry rice, dried beans, or popcorn kernels

Instructions

1. Look closely at the cardboard tube. Do you see a seam running around it? Use your marker to draw dots about half an inch apart all the way up the seam of the tube.

2. Have your adult helper poke a nail all the way in at each dot. Make sure that the nails do not poke through the other side of the tube. You will need about 30 nails from top to bottom.

3. Wrap tape around the tube to hold the nails in place.

4. Cut two circles of construction paper slightly bigger than the ends of the tube.

5. Tape one of the circles over one end of the tube. Cover it with tape so that the entire end is completely sealed.

6. Put a handful of rice, beans, or popcorn kernels into the open end of the tube.

7. Cover the open end with your hand and gently turn the tube over. How does it sound? Does it need more grains inside? Put more or less in until your rain stick sounds exactly like you want it to.

8. Place the second circle of paper over the open end of the tube. Like before, seal it with tape.

Turn the stick over and listen to the sound. Does it sound like rain falling outside your window?

15,000 to 10,000 BCE	First humans arrive in Chile from the north.
5000 BCE to 500 CE	Northern Chile has Chinchorro culture.
1450–1500	The Incas invade northern Chile.
1541	Pedro de Valdivia founds Santiago de Chile.
1567	Chiloe Island is claimed by Spain.
1722	The Dutch discover Easter Island.
1818	Chile's Declaration of Independence is signed; Santiago becomes Chile's capital.
1826	The last Spanish troops in Chile surrender; Chile's independence is complete, though still not recognized by Spain.
1834	Charles Darwin sails along the coast of Chile.
1840	Spain recognizes Chile as an independent country; diplomatic relations are established.
1879–1884	Chile defeats Peru and Bolivia in the War of the Pacific.
1946	Gabriel Gonzalez Videla becomes president.
1960	The Great Chilean earthquake strikes, killing thousands. Measuring 9.5 on the Richter scale, it is the most intense earthquake ever recorded.
1973–1989	Pinochet remains in office.
1989	Chile's first free election in 20 years is held.
1999	An economic crisis hits the region.
2003	Chile signs a free trade agreement with the United States.
2006	Chile's first female president, Michelle Bachelet, is elected.
2009	Presidential and parliamentary elections are held, but the results are too close to call.
2010	After a runoff election on January 17, Sebastián Piñera wins the majority of votes. In February, a magnitude 8.8 earthquake hits Chile and does great damage. It is the worst earthquake to hit Chile in fifty years.

Books
Burgan, Michael. *Chile.* New York: Children's Press, 2009.

Porterfield, Jason. *Chile: A Primary Source Cultural Guide.* New York: PowerPlus Books, 2003.

Schaffer. David. *Modern Nations of the World: Chile.* Farmington Hills: MI: Lucent Books, 2004.

Shields, Charles J. *Chile.* Broomall, PA: Mason Crest, 2009.

Works Consulted
Asai, Susanne, and Hubert Stadler. *Chile: A Journey Through Extremes.* Munich, Germany: Bucher, 2007.

Chester, Sharon. *A Wildlife Guide to Chile: Continental Chile, Chilean Antarctica, Easter Island, Juan Fernandez Archipelago.* Princeton, NJ: Princeton University Press, 2008.

Dorfman, Ariel, et al. *Chile: The Other September 11: An Anthology of Reflections on the 1973 Coup.* New York: Ocean Press, 2006.

Gill, Nicholas. *Travelers' Chile.* Peterborough, U.K.: Thomas Cook Publishing, 2009.

Perrone, Caterina. *Culture Smart: Chile.* New York: Random House, 2008.

Rector, John. *The History of Chile.* Basingstroke, Hampshire, England: Palgrave Macmillan, 2005.

Roraff, Susan. *Culture Shock! Chile: A Survival Guide to Customs and Etiquette.* Tarrytown, NY: Marshall Cavendish, 2007.

On the Internet
Chile from Geographia
   http://www.geographia.com/Chile/
CIA World Factbook for Chile
   https://www.cia.gov/library/publications/the-world-factbook/geos/ci.html
Lonely Planet's Chile
   http://www.lonelyplanet.com/chile
World Bank's Chile
   http://tinyurl.com/ycww7el

ahu (AH-hoo)—Stone platform.

almuerzo (al-moo-AYR-thoh)—Lunch.

ascensores (ah-sen-SOR-ayz)—Cable-like trains that travel up and down hills, carrying people between higher and lower parts of the city.

bombilla (bom-BEE-yah)—A metal drinking straw.

camanchaca (kah-mahn-CHAH-kah)—Ocean mist.

cena (THAY-nah)—Dinner.

Chileno (chee-LAY-noh)—A language that combines Spanish with German and Mapuche.

churros (CHOOR-ohs)—A cinnamon and sugar dessert.

cola de mono (KOH-lah de MOH-noh)—"Monkey's tail"; an alcoholic beverage, similar to eggnog, served at Christmas.

Cordillera de la Costa (kor-dee-YAYR-ah deh lah KOHS-tah)—Mountain range of the coast.

Criollos (kree-OH-yohs)—Spaniards who were born in Chile.

desayuno (des-ah-YOO-noh)—Breakfast.

escuela (es-KWAY-luh)—School.

Fiestas Patrias (fee-ES-tas pah-TREE-ahs)—Festival of the Home Country, which celebrates Independence Day and Armed Forces Day.

El Fin del Mundo (el FEEN del MOON-doh)—The End of the World; the southern tip of Chile.

Flor de los Andes—Flower of the Andes; a mine for the precious stone lapis lazuli.

fondas—Boarding houses.

helados (ay-LAH-dohs)—Italian-style ice cream.

Jardín Botánico Nacional (har-DEEN boh-TAH-nee-koh nah-the-oh-NAHL)—The National Botanical Gardens.

mate (mah-TAY)—Bitter tea.

media luna (MAY-de-ah LOON-ah)—"Half moon"; a corral.

moai—Volcanic rock figure or figures.

Noche de Valdivia—Valdivian Night, a celebration in a city in southern Chile.

palos de agua (pah-lohs de AHG-wah)—Stick of water; rain stick.

Parque Nacional Torres del Paine—National Park of the Paine Towers.

Parque Pumalín (PAR-kay PUH-muh-lin)—The largest private nature reserve in the world.

ramadas (RAH-mah-dahs)—Open buildings made from tree branches.

sopapillas (soh-pah-PEE-yahs)—Squares of fried dough covered in honey or sugar.

Tierra del Fuego (tee-AYR-ah del FWAY-goh)—"Land of Fire."

Viejito Pascuero—Father Christmas; Santa Claus.

Tamra Orr is a full-time author living in the Pacific Northwest. As the author of more than 250 educational books for kids of all ages, she thinks she has the best job in the world because she never stops learning. Orr has won several awards for her books, but it is her job as mother to four that she appreciates the most. She has written about more than a dozen countries across the planet, and so far Chile is the most unusual of them all.